Nefry's Kitchen

Where the Caribbean

meets the Mediterranean

By Nefretery Nancy Marin

Copyright © 2017 Nefretery Nancy Marin

All rights reserved. No part of this book may be reproduced in any form or by any electronic or mechanical means, including information storage and retrieval systems, without the express written permission of the publisher, except for the use of brief quotations in a book review.

ISBN-13: 978-1542660464

Photographs by Leo Nazim Marin. All rights reserved.

Published by Nefretery Nancy Marin.

Nefry's Kitchen

Where the Caribbean meets the Mediterranean

This book features a unique collection of exotic recipes that have withstood the test of time and been passed down through generations, mixed with original recipes that reflect the cultural melting pot of Belize.

These dishes will delight even the pickiest eaters; they are colorful, luxurious, healthy and extremely tasty. *Nefry's Kitchen* seeks to delight both the food-enthusiast and the health-conscious; as well as demonstrate that with a little imagination and a lot of culture, even the smallest budget can produce a feast!

My wish is for this book to help you have fun with simple, healthy, colorful meals that will save you money and time, while keeping your family healthy, smart and having fun at the dinner table.

Acknowledgments

I wish to express my deepest gratitude to all those who encouraged me, supported me and served as tasters in the effort to get this book published.

Special thanks to my friend and Belizean icon, Andy Palacio (RIP); writing this book was his idea, years ago, and he pushed me to do it every chance he got.

To my editor, Deb Melander, who made all of my blunders feel like important learning experiences. Every time we had to go back to the same recipe, I could feel her smile saying, "It's okay…just take your time." She eased my impatient heart. Thanks Deb!

To my husband, Jaime Marin, and my children, Xena, Leo, Jasmin and Yahzarrah, for their love, support and candid critique of my recipes.

To my best friend, Louis Diaz, for his love, continuous encouragement, constant guidance, especially his expert knowledge of liquid measures, and his unwavering help in testing recipes.

To my brother, Aaron Juan, for always being willing to run over, on short notice, to taste new recipes, never saying no to seconds and always pushing me for the next one to taste, even at the expense of breaking his life-long dieting.

To my parents, Nazim and Luzmila Juan, for their constant love and encouragement, and for teaching me that hard work and focused energy are the most important ingredients for the recipe of success.

To my sisters Marien Dela Rosa and Ninfa Juan for their love, support and honest advice.

To my many volunteers (Christina Bradic, Karen Carter, Denise V. Collins, Britney Collins, Laura Simpler, Laura Bainger, Mario Marrazzo, Adrane Jayaqumar, Emily Wilkerson, Heather Rabida, Michael Bourke, Arianna Alletzhouser, Erin Mulready and many others), who not only volunteered through my organization to assist in the development and growth of my community, but also served as testers for many of the recipes in this book. I know they are anxiously waiting to get their own copies and I thank them all for their assistance and trust in trying my recipes, for encouraging me and pushing me to "FINISH THE DAMN COOK BOOK ALREADY!"

To Leo Marin, for his love, support and dedication to the photography for this book.

Finally, I dedicate this book to the memory of my grandfather, Edwardo Juan. His exquisite cooking, his mixing of spices and knowledge of his culture were engraved in not only my heart and my memory, but never left my taste buds. I am eternally grateful for his belief in me and his investment of quality time in teaching me the importance of growing your own organic food, work ethic, respect for the diversity of cultures and ethnicity, the love of people and acceptance of their differences. Most importantly, he taught me that the heart of a united family beats from the kitchen to the dining room!

Table of Contents

Breakfast — 11

- Bread & Butter Pudding ... 13
- Breakfast Muffins ... 14
- Corn Mini Pancakes ... 15
- Creamed Couscous ... 16
- Creamed Pumpkin & Rice ... 17
- French Toast ... 18
- Hard Boiled Eggs ... 19
- Mini Pancakes ... 20
- Nefry's Eggs ... 21
- Potato Mini Pancakes ... 22

Appetizers & Snacks — 23

- Baba Ganoush ... 25
- Belizean Tamalitos ... 26
- Ceviche ... 27
- Chicken Nuggets ... 28
- Chicken Quesadilla ... 29
- Chicken Wings ... 30
- Egg Marinara ... 31
- Lasagna Rolls ... 33
- Potato Skins & Yogurt Dip ... 35
- Roasted Garlic Toast ... 36

Dinner — 37

- Egyptian Stew ... 39

Lamb Chops 40

Chicken Bel Leban 42

Chicken in Wine & Garlic 44

Quinoa & Turkey Meatballs 45

Awaal Bel-Lebanel 47

Fisherman's Fish 48

Mint Shrimp in Garlic & Butter 49

Falafel 50

Ginger & Pine Nuts Rice 51

Roast Turkey with Thyme Butter & Shallots 53

Gravy for Turkey 54

Rustic Dressing 55

Apple Salad 56

Dips & Sauces 57

Avocado & Fruit Salsa 59

Bean Dip 60

Bleu Cheese & Cashew Butter 61

Cashew Cranberry Sauce 62

Cheese Dip 63

Garlic Sauce (Tooma) 64

Guacamole 66

Hummus 67

Tahini & Yogurt Sauce 68

Breads 69

Belizean Flour Tortillas 71

Belizean Fried Jacks 72

Nancy's Bread	73
Nancy's Sweet Bread	75
Pita Bread	77

Dessert   79

Barazek	81
Belizean Lemon Pie	83
Pecan Pie	85
Sponge Cake	87

Beverages   89

Iced Hibiscus Drink	91
Lemon and Rose Punch	92
Middle Eastern Lemonade	93

Notes

Breakfast

Notes

Bread & Butter Pudding

Ingredients

2 slices wheat bread, buttered

1 1/4 cups milk

2 eggs

1 ½ teaspoons brown sugar

Pinch of ground nutmeg

Pinch of ground cinnamon

Boiling water (1 inch inside baking pan)

¼ teaspoon vanilla

Steps

Preheat oven to 350° F.

Spread butter lightly on bread; cut into small (1 inch) triangle shapes. Divide bread among four greased ½ cup baking bowls.
Whisk milk, eggs, sugar, and vanilla in a bowl. Pour egg mixture over bread; sprinkle with nutmeg and cinnamon. Place the small bowls in a larger baking pan. Pour boiling water into larger pan to a depth of 1 in. Cover with foil and bake for 20 minutes; uncover and bake for additional 5 minutes, or until mixture is firm.

Breakfast Muffins

Ingredients

4 eggs, beaten

1 ½ tablespoons butter

¼ cup milk

½ teaspoon baking powder

2 ounces turkey ham, finely chopped

2 small button mushrooms, finely chopped

1 ½ tablespoons tomatoes, finely chopped

½ tablespoons onions, finely chopped

½ tablespoons sweet pepper, finely chopped

½ tablespoons cilantro, finely chopped

3 tablespoons cheddar cheese, grated

Steps

Preheat oven to 350º F.

Beat eggs, in a bowl; add in melted butter, milk, turkey ham, baking powder, and beat well.

Grease muffin pans. Place chopped veggies and cheese inside each muffin cup, then pour in egg mixture, only filling each muffin cup halfway. Place in oven and bake for 8 minutes or until lightly browned.

Serve with tortillas or toast.

Makes 12 muffins.

Corn Mini Pancakes

Ingredients

1 cup flour

1 teaspoon baking powder

¾ cup milk

1 egg

1 ½ tablespoons butter, melted

4 ½ ounces (½ cup) canned creamed corn

2 green onions, finely chopped

¼ cup sweet pepper, finely chopped

¼ cup cheddar cheese, grated

Steps

Place flour and baking powder in a bowl; stir in milk, egg, butter, and mix to a smooth batter. Stir in remaining ingredients.

Pre-heat comal (griddle) at medium heat, Drop a tablespoon full onto greased comal (griddle) and cook until bubbles appear; turn pancakes on other side and cook until lightly brown.

Serve with cream cheese or goat cheese.

Makes 8 mini pancakes.

Creamed Couscous

Ingredients

¾ cup milk

1 ½ tablespoons couscous

1 tablespoon condensed milk

Pinch of cinnamon

Steps

Combine all ingredients in a small saucepan, cook at medium temperature until couscous is cooked; then reduce to simmer, stirring frequently, for about 12 minutes or until thickened.

Serve with sliced banana.

Makes 2 servings.

Creamed Pumpkin & Rice

Ingredients

½ cup cow or goat milk

2 tablespoons condensed milk

1 small fresh pumpkin (white crookneck pumpkin, or Tennessee Sweet Potato Squash varieties are the types that work best)

¼ cup long grain, uncooked white rice or black rice (keep in mind that black rice will change the color and add a slightly sweeter taste)

2 sticks cinnamon

Steps

Pour milk into a saucepan and bring to a boil; stir in pumpkin and cinnamon sticks. Cook at medium temperature until pumpkin is tender. Stir in rice and lower the temperature slightly. Cook, stirring frequently, about 5 minutes, or until thickened. Sweeten with condensed milk. Serve in bowls (you may leave cinnamon sticks in as a garnish if you wish).

Suggest serving with fresh fruit or berries.

Makes 2 servings.

French Toast

Ingredients

4 eggs, beaten

½ can full cream milk

2 tablespoons sugar

1 tablespoon vanilla

½ teaspoon cinnamon

6 slices whole wheat bread

Steps

Preheat stove top comal (or electric griddle) for about 3 minutes and spray with non-stick spray or butter (if needed).

Beat eggs in a bowl; add milk, sugar, vanilla, cinnamon, and beat well.

Dip individual slices of bread in batter until soaked. Place slice of soaked bread on hot buttered comal (griddle) and brown on both sides.

Serve with cream cheese, maple syrup (or natural honey) and sliced bananas

Hard Boiled Eggs

Ingredients

½ tablespoon onion, finely chopped

½ of a small ripe tomato

2 eggs, hardboiled

Small drop of coconut oil (could substitute butter or regular cooking oil)

Dash of salt & pepper

Steps

Preheat oil in sauce pan for about 1 minute on low heat.

Peel and slice the tomato ½ inch thick.

Sauté onion in oil until softened, then add tomato, salt and pepper and cook for 10 minutes over low heat.

Shell eggs, leave whole, and slide into the tomato mixture. Cook for 5 minutes.

To serve, remove the eggs, cut in half, then arrange on a serving plate and cover with tomato mixture.

Mini Pancakes

Ingredients

1 cup flour

½ teaspoon baking powder

3 tablespoons brown sugar

1 egg, lightly beaten

¾ cup milk (add a little more if needed)

2 tablespoons vanilla essence

Steps

Preheat stove top comal (or electric griddle) for about 3 minutes and spray with nonstick spray or butter (if needed).

Combine flour, baking powder, and sugar in a medium bowl; gradually whisk in egg and enough milk to create a thick, smooth batter.

Drop a tablespoon full of batter onto greased comal (griddle) and cook until bubbles appear on the surface of the pancakes. Flip, and lightly brown the other side.

Serve with yogurt and diced fruit on top; drizzle with honey.

Makes about 20 mini pancakes.

Nefry's Eggs

Ingredients

2 eggs, beaten

1 ½ tablespoons butter

1 ½ tablespoons milk

2 ounces turkey ham, finely chopped

2 small button mushrooms, finely chopped

1 ½ tablespoons tomatoes, finely chopped

½ tablespoon onions, finely chopped

½ tablespoon sweet pepper, finely chopped

½ tablespoon cilantro, finely chopped

3 tablespoons cheddar cheese, grated

Steps

In a small frying pan heat butter. Stir in ham, mushrooms and veggies, stirring for about 3 minutes or until ham and onions are browned.

In a small bowl, combine eggs, cilantro and milk; whisk until egg mixture is fluffy. Stir into meat and veggie mixture. Stir in cheese and cook at low temperature, until mixture sets.

Serve with buttered toast.

Makes 2 servings.

Potato Mini Pancakes

Ingredients

1 cup flour

1 teaspoon baking powder

¾ cup milk

1 egg

1 ½ tablespoons butter, melted

1 clove garlic, crushed

1 small onion, coarsely grated

1 small potato, coarsely grated

Steps

Preheat stove top comal (or electric griddle) for about 3 minutes and spray with non-stick spray or butter (if needed).

Place flour and baking powder in a bowl; stir in milk, egg, butter, and mix to a smooth batter. Stir in remaining ingredients.

Drop a tablespoon full onto greased comal (griddle) and cook until bubbles appear; turn pancakes on other side and cook until lightly brown.

Serve with cream cheese or goat cheese.

Makes 8 mini pancakes.

Appetizers & Snacks

Notes

Baba Ganoush

Ingredients

4 to 6 medium sized, dark skinned eggplant

1 teaspoon olive oil

5 teaspoon tahini (sesame seed paste)

1 teaspoon garlic, chopped

1/2 teaspoon cumin seed powder

1 tablespoon lemon juice

Salt to taste

1 teaspoon coriander (cilantro), chopped for garnish

Oil for greasing

Steps

Grease the eggplants with a little oil, place whole on a baking tray and bake in pre-heated oven at 350° until the skin is charred and the eggplant is tender (approximately 20 minutes).

Cool, peel and discard the skin and mash the eggplant to a pulp.

Add all the remaining ingredients and mix well.

Garnish with coriander (cilantro) and serve with toasted pita bread slices or tortilla chips.

Belizean Tamalitos

Ingredients

8 ears fresh green corn

1 small onion

1 small bell pepper

½ cup coconut milk

2 sticks margarine or butter, melted

½ teaspoon thyme (I usually use fresh thyme as best I can but may substitute with dried when fresh is not available)

¼ cups evaporated milk

½ teaspoon salt

½ teaspoon sugar

2 teaspoons baking powder

Steps

First, husk the corn, making sure to save some of the greener leaves and place them aside.

In a bowl, slice corn kernels off the cob, blend or grind corn, onion, bell pepper and all other ingredients. Then, take the husks you saved and spoon about 2 ½ tablespoons of mixture on each husk. Wrap the tamale, folding one end and leaving the other end open. Place them, standing upright, in a deep pot or steamer, until tightly stacked.

 Lastly, cover the tamalitos with some corn husks and fill pot half way with water, so as to avoid water from entering the tamalitos. Cover and place pot on high heat for 1 to 1 1/2 hours.

Ceviche

Ingredients

8-12 ounces fresh shrimp (properly cleaned and washed with lime juice)

4-6 tablespoons lime juice

Salt and pepper to taste

1 large red onion, finely diced

2 large tomatoes, finely diced

1 large bell pepper

4 cloves garlic, finely chopped

½ teaspoon dried chilies

1 cup cilantro, finely chopped

Steps

Combine lime juice, salt and pepper, diced tomatoes, garlic, bell pepper, red onion and cilantro; in a deep bowl and mix well. Dice shrimp and add to the mixture. Let sit in the refrigerator for 3-4 hours turning occasionally to coat. Sprinkle with chilies and serve with tortilla chips.

Chicken Nuggets

Ingredients

1 slice white bread

6 ounces boneless chicken breast, chopped

¼ cup finely grated cheese (I use a mix of cheddar and mozzarella)

1 egg yolk

1 small potato, grated

1 small onion, grated

1 teaspoon poultry seasoning (or just salt and pepper works fine)

Half head of garlic

3 tablespoon packaged breadcrumbs

Vegetable oil for frying

Steps

Blend or process bread, chicken, and cheese until combined; transfer to a medium bowl. Add egg, potato, onion and seasoning (or salt and pepper); mix well. Shape rounded tablespoon of mixture into nuggets; roll in breadcrumbs.

Deep fry nuggets: Add oil to a deep pot, but fill it no more than half full. Generally the walls of the pot should rise at least 10 cm. (4 in.) above the oil so that there are no spillovers. This also helps contain splattering and makes cleanup easier. Use enough oil so that you can submerge a small batch of nuggets completely.

Preheat the oil to 375° F. Fry nuggets in batches until chicken is cooked through and golden brown; drain on paper towel and pat dry until excess oil is controlled.

Chicken Quesadilla

Ingredients

1 small tomato, diced

1 small green bell pepper, sliced round (remove seeds)

1 small white onion, sliced round

½ teaspoon olive oil

½ handful mozzarella cheese

4 single black olives, pitted and sliced

½ tablespoon sliced jalapeno pepper

1 grilled chicken breast, shredded

1 large flour tortilla

Steps

Preheat griddle on medium heat for about 5 minutes.

Place tomato, onion, bell pepper and shredded grilled chicken breast on hot griddle and sprinkle with olive oil. Cook until tender, about 15 minutes.

Cut flour tortilla into wedges and place on a plate. Spread chicken, and grilled veggies evenly on tortilla wedges.

Sprinkle the mozzarella cheese on top and place in microwave for 1 minute, so that the cheese can melt.

Sprinkle olives and jalapeno pepper on top and serve with sour cream.

Chicken Wings

Ingredients

1 clove garlic, crushed

3 tablespoons soy sauce

2 tablespoons dry sherry

2 tablespoons barbeque sauce

2 tablespoons honey

2 tablespoons ginger, grated

1 tablespoon sesame oil

12 chicken wings, thoroughly washed

1 tablespoon sesame seeds, toasted

Steps

For stovetop toasting, use a wide frying pan. Heat the sesame seeds on medium heat, shaking the pan occasionally. Remove the seeds when they darken and become fragrant, then set aside.

In a large bowl, place garlic, soy sauce, sherry, barbeque sauce, honey, ginger, and sesame oil; using a fork, mix the ingredients together evenly.

Add the chicken wings to the marinade and toss thoroughly to coat. Cover the bowl with plastic wrap and refrigerate for 30 minutes or longer.

Preheat grill for about 5 minutes on medium heat.

Cook the chicken wings on a fairly hot grill for 20 -25 minutes, turning occasionally and basting with the remaining marinade.

Sprinkle the chicken wings with sesame seeds and serve on their own as an appetizer or side dish, or as a light meal with crisp green salad.

Egg Marinara

Ingredients

For Marinara:

4 tablespoon extra-virgin olive oil

1 medium onion, coarsely chopped

3 cloves garlic, thinly sliced

1 teaspoon hot chili flakes

1 (14-ounce) can crushed tomatoes

½ cup fresh Basil, shredded

A sprinkle of salt and pepper

Just a tiny pinch of sugar

Additional Items:

4 large eggs

¼ cup grated cheddar cheese

Steps

For Marinara:

Preheat olive oil in a sauce pan over medium-high heat.

Sauté onions in olive oil, until tender; add garlic, crushed tomatoes, chili flakes and basil and cook over medium heat for 5 minutes, stirring constantly.

Add salt, pepper and sugar to taste. Keep stirring over lowered heat for another 3 minutes.

When marinara is done, let it cool.

Pre-heat oven to 325° F. Spoon about 3 ounces of marinara into 4 individual terra cotta baking dishes. Place 1 cracked egg in the center of each marinara dish, sprinkle cheddar cheese on top and bake for 2 to 5 minutes - depending on how you like your eggs.

Lasagna Rolls

Ingredients

1 lb. lasagna noodles, uncooked

Filling:

15 ounces ricotta

½ cup shredded mozzarella

¼ cup grated parmesan

2 tablespoons chopped fresh parsley

2 large garlic cloves, minced

1 (10 ounce) bag fresh spinach, cooked and thoroughly squeezed dry, then chopped.

1 large egg

Topping:

1½ cups marinara

1 cup shredded mozzarella

¼ cup shredded parmesan

Salt and pepper to taste

Steps

Preheat oven to 400° F.

Fill a large pot ¾ full with water and bring to a boil over high heat. When it starts to boil, toss in a handful of salt, followed by the lasagna noodles.

While the noodles are boiling, prepare the filling. Mix together the ricotta, ½ cup mozzarella, ¼ cup parmesan, garlic, egg, and spinach until well combined. Set aside until the noodles are ready.

Boil the lasagna noodles until still partially raw but pliable, about 10 minutes (I do it this way because I think the noodles stick together and tear more when they are fully cooked. They will finish cooking later in the oven.) Remove the noodles and separate them when they're cool enough to handle.

Lay one noodle on a flat surface. Spread a spoonful of the filling evenly over the noodle, leaving a ½ inch edge on one end so when you roll it up, the bare edge can seal the roll together.

Spray a 9x13 baking pan with non-stick spray. Spread about ¾ cup of marinara on the bottom of the pan, completely covering with the sauce. Place your finished lasagna roll in the pan on top of the sauce. Repeat the filling and rolling process with the remaining lasagna noodles.

Once all of the lasagna noodles have been filled and rolled and placed in the baking pan, cover the rolls completely with the rest of the marinara, then sprinkle the 1 cup mozzarella and ¼ cup parmesan on top. Cover the pan with aluminum foil, then bake for 30 minutes or until the noodles are tender and the cheese is melted. Uncover and bake another 5-8 minutes, if you want the cheese on top to brown.

Potato Skins & Yogurt Dip

Ingredients

4 large baking potatoes, washed

Olive oil for brushing

1 cup plain (natural) yogurt

2 cloves garlic, crushed

2 teaspoons tomato paste

1 teaspoon green chili, chopped

½ teaspoon celery salt

Salt and freshly ground black pepper

Steps

Preheat oven to 350º F.

Bake the potatoes for about 45 minutes or until tender. Cut in half lengthwise and scoop out the flesh, leaving a thin layer of flesh on the skins. The removed potato flesh can be reserved in the refrigerator or freezer for another meal.

Preheat grill on medium-high. Cut each potato shell in half lengthwise again and lightly brush the skin with olive oil. Cook skins on a medium-hot grill for 4-5 minutes, or until crisp.

To make the dip, mix together the remaining ingredients in a bowl, adding salt and pepper to taste. Serve potato skins with yogurt dip on the side.

Roasted Garlic Toast

Ingredients

2 whole garlic heads

1 tablespoon extra-virgin olive oil

5 sprigs fresh rosemary (1 sprig, chopped, and set aside for garnish)

Loaf of freshly baked bread

Salt

Freshly ground black pepper

Steps

Preheat grill on medium heat for about 5 minutes.

Slice the tops from the heads of garlic using a sharp knife.

Brush the garlic with olive oil and add a few springs of fresh rosemary before wrapping garlic heads in foil. Cook foil-wrapped garlic on a medium-hot grill for 25-30 minutes, turning occasionally, until the garlic is soft.

Slice the bread into ½ inch slices and brush each slice generously with olive oil. Toast slices on the grill until crisp and golden, turning once.

Squeeze the garlic cloves from their skins onto the toast. Sprinkle with the chopped fresh rosemary and olive oil, then add salt and black pepper to taste, and spread on toast.

Dinner

Notes

Meats

Egyptian Stew

Ingredients

2 cups vegetable oil

8 chives, skin removed

1 pound of stewing beef, 1-inch cubed

3 large carrots, diced small

1 cup hot water

3 cloves garlic, crushed with salt

Salt and pepper

Steps

Heat the oil in a frying pan over medium heat, and brown the chives. Once browned, put the chives into a stew pan on top of the stove; leave the oil in the frying pan on medium heat and brown the steak in the same oil. Remove the steak and add to the chives.

Brown the carrots in the same oil and add both the carrots and the oil to the steak and chives. Add hot water along with garlic, salt and pepper to taste.

Put the lid on the stew pan and simmer for two hours, over low heat. Replenish with small amounts of water if needed, but let the liquid reduce to make a rich sauce.

Lamb Chops

Ingredients

1 cup plain yogurt

¼ cup fresh lemon juice

1 tablespoon ground dried chilies (such as jalapeno) or chili powder

2 ½ tablespoons ground cardamom

½ cup olive oil, divided

12 lamb rib chops (about 4 ounces each)

Salt and ground black pepper

½ cup tahini & yogurt sauce (see recipe on page…)

¼ cup cilantro

Steps

Mix the yogurt, ground chilies, cardamom and ¼ cup olive oil in a shallow non-reactive dish, large enough to hold all the lamb chops tightly in one layer.

Add the lamb chops, cover and refrigerate for 24 hours, turning once.

Remove the lamb from the marinade, scraping off any marinade from the chops. Brush with 2 tablespoons of the remaining oil and season with salt, pepper and lemon juice.

Put the last 2 tablespoons of oil in a large heavy-bottomed skillet over medium-high heat. Cook the chops for 3-4 minutes per side for medium rare. Lamb should be slightly springy to the touch and the juice reddish-pink. You will have to do this in batches if cooking for more than 3 persons.

Cover cooked chops with foil to keep warm. Allow chops to rest for 3 to 4 minutes.

Arrange two chops per plate, overlapping in a semicircle. Drizzle with tahini & yogurt sauce, then garnish with cilantro leaves on top.

Poultry

Chicken Bel Leban

Ingredients

¾ cup corn oil

2 onions, finely chopped

1 chicken, cut into pieces at the joints

½ tablespoon ground coriander

½ tablespoon ground black pepper

2 chili peppers, split

1 cup plain yogurt

¼ cup water

Salt

Steps

Preheat oil in a saucepan to 350°F. Add onions and cook till soft; add the chicken and stir.

Add spices, the chili peppers, and salt; Cover and cook over low heat, for approximately 18 minutes, stirring occasionally and adding water as required.

In a separate pan, over low heat, whisk the yogurt and water together. Bring to a boil, stirring constantly. Remove the yogurt from the heat and set aside.

When the chicken is cooked, add the yogurt and simmer on low heat for about 5 minutes.

Serve in a deep dish along with white rice.

Chicken in Wine & Garlic

Ingredients

4 large boneless skinless chicken breasts

5 tablespoons olive oil

1 onion, finely chopped

6 garlic cloves, finely chopped

4 tablespoons white wine

4 tablespoons parsley, chopped

4 tablespoons cilantro, chopped

Salt and pepper

Steps

Wash chicken well with lemons or vinegar. Slice chicken into thin slices.

Heat the olive oil in a large heavy-bottom skillet over medium-high heat; add onion, and cook for 5 minutes, or until softened, but not browned. Add garlic and cook for additional 30 seconds.

Add the sliced chicken to the skillet and cook gently for 5-10 minutes, stirring from time to time, until all ingredients are lightly browned and the chicken is tender.

Add the wine and let it bubble and deglaze the skillet, scraping up all the bits. Add the parsley and cilantro, and season with salt and pepper, to taste. Transfer chicken and sauce to a warm serving dish.

Garnish with lemon wedges and serve with rice or potato dish.

Quinoa & Turkey Meatballs

Ingredients

Meatballs:

1 1/2 pounds extra-lean ground turkey

2 cups cooked quinoa

1 egg

1/3 cup chopped green onions

1/3 cup chopped basil

2 cups cilantro

1 tablespoon fennel seeds

1 tablespoon Italian seasoning

1 cup olive oil

Pinch of salt to taste

Sauce:

3 garlic cloves, thinly sliced

1 can (32 ounce) whole tomatoes, in juice

2 bay leaves

4 oregano sprigs

1 rosemary sprig

Kosher salt

Freshly ground black pepper

Parmesan cheese, for serving

Steps

Mix all ingredients in a mixing bowl. In a large heavy skillet, heat the oil over medium heat until hot. Form the turkey mixture into twelve 2-inch meatballs. Brown the meatballs in two batches, turning once, until golden brown; about 5 to 7 minutes per batch. Transfer to a platter as browned. Discard all but 2 tablespoons of the frying oil.

MAKE THE SAUCE in the skillet used to brown the meatballs. Heat the reserved 2 tablespoons oil over medium-high heat until hot, then stir in the garlic and cook until golden, about 4 minutes. Stir in the tomatoes, bay leaves, oregano, rosemary and ½ teaspoon each salt and pepper. Simmer the sauce, stirring and breaking the tomatoes up with a spoon, until slightly thickened, about 8 minutes. Add the meatballs to the skillet and continue to simmer until the meatballs are cooked through, 10 to 12 minutes. Serve the meatballs with the sauce, over pasta or with rice; sprinkle with parmesan.

You may even make these into patties, grill and serve in a sandwich.

Seafood

Awaal Bel-Lebanel

Ingredients

2 pounds jumbo shrimp, cleaned

Marinade:

1 cup low fat yogurt

½ teaspoon curry powder, cumin or allspice

¼ teaspoon red pepper

Pinch black pepper

2 cloves garlic, crushed with salt

Skewers

Steps

Combine the marinade ingredients in a large mixing bowl. Add the shrimp and turn to coat each piece with the marinade. Cover and refrigerate for 2 hours or longer.

Thread marinated shrimp onto skewers and grill over medium-high heat, basting with the remaining marinade; approximately 2 minutes on each side.

Serving suggestions include: fresh garden salad, grilled potatoes - or my favorite, Ginger & Pine Nuts Rice (see page 43 for recipe).

Fisherman's Fish

Ingredients

4 tablespoons olive oil

3 medium onions, finely chopped

1 ½ pints water

1 teaspoon salt

1 teaspoon ground cumin

2 ¼ pounds snapper fillets

1 pound long grain rice

2 ounces pine nuts

1 lemon, juiced

Steps

Heat 3 tablespoons of oil in a large saucepan over medium heat, and sauté the onions for about 3 minutes, or until brown. Add water, salt and cumin, and simmer until onions have become very soft.

Add fish and cook gently for 10 minutes. Remove fish and keep warm.

Use approximately 2 cups of the stock in which the fish has been cooked combined with the water to cook the rice; place stock and rice in a separate pan, and cook until the rice is tender and stock absorbed.

Spoon the rice into a shallow dish and lay the fish pieces on top.

Sauté the pine nuts in remaining tablespoon of oil until slightly brown, and scatter them over the fish.

Meanwhile, simmer and reduce the remaining stock, adding the lemon juice. Pour sauce over the fish and rice. Serve.

Mint Shrimp in Garlic & Butter

Ingredients

1 pound jumbo shrimp, uncooked

2 lemons, juiced

1 bunch mint, chopped (Save a sprinkle of mint for the garnish)

4 garlic cloves, finely chopped

2 ounces butter

Steps

Shell and devein shrimp. Place in a shallow dish with lemon juice, mint and garlic; toss well to coat. Cover and let marinate for 30 minutes.

Remove the shrimp and sauté in olive oil until they turn pink and are cooked through, about 3 minutes. Add the marinade to saucepan.

Serve hot with a sprinkle of mint.

Vegetarian

Falafel

Ingredients

1 1/3 cups chickpeas (precooked or canned)

1 large onion, finely chopped

2 garlic cloves, grated

Salt and cayenne pepper (just a pinch)

2 tablespoons fresh parsley, chopped

2 tablespoons cilantro, chopped

2 teaspoons ground cumin

2 teaspoons ground coriander

½ teaspoon baking powder

Vegetable oil for deep frying

Steps

Place chickpeas in food processor or blender and process to make a coarse paste. Add the onion, garlic, seasoning, parsley, cilantro, spices and baking powder; process again to mix well. Let mixture rest for 30 minutes, then divide into 8 equal pieces. Shape into ball between palms of hands. Let them rest for 30 minutes.

Heat oil to 350°F for deep frying in a wok or deep pan. Gently drop the balls into the oil and cook until golden brown. Carefully remove from the oil and drain for a few minutes on a plate lined with paper towel.

(Serve with humus dip and pita bread)

Ginger & Pine Nuts Rice

Ingredients

1 cup white rice

1 tablespoon coconut oil (or oil of choice)

2 large cloves garlic, minced

1 tablespoon ginger, peeled and grated

1 teaspoon turmeric

½ cup carrots, grated

1 small onion, diced

¾ teaspoon salt

2 cups boiling water

1 tablespoon fresh lemon juice

½ cup dried cranberries or raisins

¼ cup fresh cilantro, chopped

¼ cup pine nuts

Steps

Pour the dry rice into a bowl and cover with cool water. Soak for 15 minutes, then drain.

While rice is soaking, put on a kettle of water and bring to a full boil.

Add the coconut oil, garlic, and ginger to a medium-sized pot and heat to medium. Sauté until very fragrant, about 3 minutes.

Add the onion, carrots, pine nuts, cilantro, turmeric and salt and sauté in the hot oil for an additional 2 to 3 minutes; set aside.

A few minutes before rice is finished cooking, stir the fresh lemon juice and dried cranberries into the rice. Then add the sautéed mixture and stir into the rice, making sure to stir from the bottom up, so the rice gets that yellowish color from the turmeric. Replace the cover and continue to cook over very low heat for another 3 minutes.

Serve alongside your favorite main dish.

Christmas Special

Roast Turkey with Thyme Butter & Shallots

Ingredients

1 (14 pound) turkey, thawed

Salt & black pepper

¾ cup unsalted butter, softened

2 tablespoons fresh thyme, chopped

12 large shallots, finely chopped

2 tablespoon olive oil

1 head garlic, minced

Steps

Preheat oven to 400º F.

Combine all ingredients and apply under turkey skin and on top.

Put prepared turkey in oven, bake for 20 minutes to brown it. Reduce oven heat to 325º F and roast for two hours, basting periodically. Reduce heat further, to 225º F, until turkey is done – approximately 30 minutes to an hour more. Remove from oven and let the turkey rest before carving.

Gravy for Turkey

Ingredients

½ cup all-purpose flour

½ cup reserved pan drippings from roasted turkey

1 ½ cups turkey or chicken broth (I make this out of the entrails of the turkey)

¾ teaspoon salt

¾ teaspoon black pepper

Steps

Brown the flour in saucepan, over medium heat; add all remaining ingredients and stir until thick.

Rustic Dressing

Ingredients

1 can whole kernel corn (drained)

1 pound smoked turkey bacon

2 cups chopped onion

2 cups chopped bell pepper

1 ½ cups chopped celery

4 cloves garlic

½ cup butter (melted)

6 cups packaged stuffing

1 ½ cups chopped pecans

1 large egg, beaten lightly

2 to 2 ¾ cup broth (turkey or chicken)

½ teaspoon salt

1 teaspoon black pepper

Steps

Combine all ingredients and sauté in a large skillet for four minutes, over medium heat. Midway through roasting, stuff your turkey. Place the stuffed turkey back in the oven to continue roasting until done, then serve.

Apple Salad

Ingredients

5 to 6 apples (both red and green), cored and chopped

4 stalks celery, chopped

1 cup pecans, chopped

1 cup pitted dates (use raisins if you cannot find dates or don't like them), chopped

1 cup mayonnaise

2 tablespoons sugar

2 tablespoons milk

Steps

Combine all ingredients in a salad bowl and serve.

Dips & Sauces

Notes

Avocado & Fruit Salsa

Ingredients

1 mango, peeled, seeded and diced (when not available I substitute with pineapple or red apples; sometimes I get daring and just use all the above fruits)

1 avocado, peeled, pitted and diced

4 medium tomatoes, diced

1 jalapeno pepper, seeded and minced

½ cup fresh cilantro, chopped

3 cloves garlic, minced

1 teaspoon salt

2 tablespoons fresh lime juice

¼ cup red onion, chopped

3 tablespoons coconut oil (could be done with olive oil, if you cannot find coconut oil)

Steps

In a medium bowl, combine the mango, avocado, tomatoes, jalapeno, cilantro, and garlic. Stir in the salt, lime juice, red onion, and olive oil. To blend the flavors, refrigerate for about 30 minutes before serving.

Bean Dip

Ingredients

1 can (16 ounce) refried beans (this could be homemade instead of canned too)

1 large onion, diced

1 large bell pepper, diced

1 large tomato, chopped

1 clove garlic, grated

¼ cup black olives, drained and sliced (for garnish)

2 small cans (7 oz.) Herdez brand Salsa Casera

2 tablespoons coconut oil

Steps

In a shallow sauce pan, heat the coconut oil and stir fry the onions, bell pepper and garlic. When these are browned, add in the tomatoes and the refried beans and cook for about 2 minutes; then add in the Salsa Casera, stirring constantly.

Serve the bean dip in a deep bowl and add the olive slices to garnish.

Bleu Cheese & Cashew Butter

Ingredients

20 ounces unsalted butter, divided

4 scallions, finely chopped

5 ounces bleu cheese (use your favorite), chopped

2 tablespoons finely chopped cashew nuts (walnuts work too)

3 stems cilantro, finely chopped

Steps

Melt half the butter in a skillet, add the scallions and cook over low heat, stirring frequently for a few minutes until softened.

Transfer to a bowl and mix in the remaining butter, bleu cheese, cilantro and nuts. Form into a log then cover and let chill until required.

Cashew Cranberry Sauce

Ingredients

1 can whole berry cranberry sauce

1/3 cup strawberry preserves

1 ½ tablespoons sugar

¼ teaspoon ground cinnamon

½ cup coarsely chopped cashew nuts, toasted

1 tablespoon balsamic vinegar or red wine (I use a pinot noir, you can use your preferred wine)

Steps

In a sauce pan, heat cranberry sauce, strawberry preserves and wine over low heat. As the mixture starts to simmer, add in sugar, cinnamon and cashew nuts.

Serve with your Thanksgiving or Christmas turkey or your favorite poultry dish (a perfect match with roast duck).

Cheese Dip

Ingredients

1 lb. processed cheese (I use Happy Cow cheese in Belize), chopped

1 large can (12.69 oz.) evaporated milk

1 medium onion, chopped

1 small bell pepper, chopped

4 cloves garlic, chopped

1 small can (7 oz.) Herdez brand Salsa Casera

Add jalapeno pepper to taste (this is optional, I do not use it for the children)

Steps

Blend all ingredients together using a food processor until consistency is smooth or blended to your liking. You can add more evaporated milk as desired for less thickness.

Serve with tortilla chips, nachos or pita chips

Garlic Sauce (Tooma)

Ingredients

3 heads of garlic, peeled
4-5 cups of vegetable oil (canola/sunflower/peanut etc.)
1 lemon, freshly juiced
1 teaspoon of salt (or to taste)

Steps

Before you start, ensure that all ingredients are at room temperature for a more reliable outcome. Also if you are using a large food processor make sure you use at least 3 heads of garlic otherwise smaller quantities of garlic may not be reached by the blades.

Add the garlic and salt to the food processor and run for 10-20 seconds. Stop processor, scrape garlic down the sides, then run processor again for another 10-20 seconds. Repeat 3-4 times until garlic starts to turn pasty and looks crushed. This is very important to reach before proceeding.

At this point, turn the processor back on and keep it on until the end. Start adding the oil to the processor at a very slow rate, in a very thin stream, about ½ cup at a time. After adding the first ½ cup you will start seeing the garlic emulsify and turn into a paste.
Add ½ teaspoon of lemon juice very slowly, in a thin stream. Wait a few seconds until the lemon juice is well absorbed; repeat the same process - slowly adding ½ cup of oil, waiting a few seconds, then adding ½ teaspoon of lemon juice - until you've used all ingredients. This process should take 8-10 minutes.

If at any point you see that the paste is turning liquid, it may be an indication that you've added either too much lemon juice, or oil, or you may have added them at a fast rate. In this case your options may be limited especially if the paste completely breaks. Sometimes adding a cube of ice may help.

Notes:

Don't use heavy oils like olive, avocado or sesame seed, as they give a strong and bitter taste to the garlic. Use lighter oil such as safflower, sunflower, canola, or vegetable.

If the resulting garlic paste is too strong, you could either mix it with a mashed medium size baked (or boiled) potato, or you can increase the amount of oil.

You could also add a small pinch of citric acid in the beginning, with the garlic and salt, to give the paste more tang.

Guacamole

Ingredients

3 avocados, peeled, pitted and mashed

1 lime, juiced

1 teaspoon salt

1 medium onion, diced

1 medium bell pepper, diced

3 tablespoons fresh cilantro, chopped

2 large tomatoes, diced

2 cloves garlic, minced

1 pinch ground black pepper (optional)

Steps

In a medium bowl, mash together the avocados, lime juice, and salt. Mix in onion, cilantro, tomatoes, and garlic. Stir in black pepper. Refrigerate 1 hour for best flavor, or serve immediately.

Hummus

Ingredients

2 teaspoons tahini (bottled sesame paste)

1 medium lemon, juiced (or more as needed, to taste)

3 cloves garlic

Salt to taste

1 large can (12.69 oz.) evaporated milk

1 cup of canned chickpeas

¼ hot pepper (jalapeño, habanero, etc.) or red pepper flakes

Fresh parsley, chopped (for garnish)

Olive oil (for garnish)

Steps

Place tahini into blender or food processor, add lemon juice and puree; add garlic, some salt, evaporated milk and blend some more. Add chickpeas and pepper (optional) and continue blending until smooth and to your preferred taste.

To serve place the hummus on a plate and spread out with a spoon; sprinkle with parsley and drizzle olive oil on top.

Tahini & Yogurt Sauce

Ingredients

2 teaspoon tahini (bottled sesame paste)

1 medium lemon, juiced (more as needed, to taste)

3 cloves garlic

Salt to taste

1 cup low fat plain yogurt

Fresh parsley, chopped (for garnish)

Olive oil (for garnish)

Steps

Place tahini into blender or food processor, add lemon juice, and puree; add garlic, some salt, and blend. Add yogurt and continue blending until smooth and to your preferred taste.

To serve, place the sauce on a plate and spread out with a spoon; sprinkle with parsley and drizzle olive oil on top.

Breads

Notes

Belizean Flour Tortillas

Ingredients

2 lbs. flour (I do 1 lb. white flour and 1 lb. whole wheat, but it can be done with all white)

6 teaspoons baking powder

1 teaspoon salt

¼ lb. shortening

¼ lb. butter

1 cup Grace Coconut powder

2 teaspoons chia seeds

Water to moisten

Steps

Place all ingredients in a bowl except water. Add enough water to moisten. Knead lightly until dough forms. Cut dough into 10 pieces and form small balls. Leave dough to swell for about 15 mins. Flatten balls with hand or rolling pin. Bake on stove top using iron griddle or Comal over low heat. Cook for 3-4 minutes on each side.

Belizean Fried Jacks

Ingredients

3 cups flour

3 teaspoons baking powder

1 teaspoon salt

1 package coconut milk powder

1 teaspoon shortening (for the dough)

1 cup water (sometimes water might need to be adjusted)

2 cups vegetable oil (for cooking)

Steps

Place flour, baking powder, coconut milk powder and salt in a bowl. Cut shortening into flour or knead the dough, adding small amounts of warm water at a time, in order to remove all clumps and create a smooth textured dough. Separate the dough in half and let stand for about 15 minutes.

Pour vegetable oil in the frying pan and heat to medium-high temperature. Cut dough into ten medium-sized balls and flatten them into a circle. Cut each circle in half. Place dough in the frying pan and leave until it turns golden brown. Dough must be turned in the oil until golden brown on both sides

Nancy's Bread

Ingredients

2 cups flour (I do 1 cup white flour and 1 cup whole wheat, but it can be done with all white)

2/3 teaspoon salt

2 tablespoons sugar

1 tablespoon instant yeast

¾ cup coconut milk

1 tablespoon shortening or margarine

1 tablespoon butter

2 eggs

Steps

In a deep bowl, mix flour, sugar and all other dry ingredients together. Make a hole in the center.

Melt shortening or margarine in a pot, add evaporated milk and (warm slightly on stove top). Do not boil.

Add yeast to warm milk. Add milk mixture to flour (pour it in the center of the hole you created in the flour mixture). Mix with your clean hands until it holds together, knead and let rise for about 20 minutes or until dough swells up.

Knead again on a floured board.

Cut into 6-8 pieces. Form into round balls or whatever shape and size you like. Flatten slightly. Put in greased baking pan. Let rise until doubled in size.

Preheat oven 350º to 375º F (180º C).

Bake for 30-40 minutes until brown all over or has hollow sound when tapped on the bottom. Cool on wire rack.

Enjoy!

Nancy's Sweet Bread

Ingredients

2 lbs. all-purpose bread flour (8 cups)

2 tablespoons instant yeast

2 teaspoons sugar

1 egg, beaten

4 ounces shortening (1/2 cup) or 1 ½ sticks margarine

1 teaspoon ground cinnamon

½ - ¾ lb. brown sugar (1 cup)

¾ cup warm water

2 teaspoon vanilla

1 ½ cups evaporated milk

1 cup raisins or dried cranberries (optional)

½ cup dried apricots

½ tablespoon ground flax seed

½ tablespoon chia seeds

1 cup mixed nuts (I use seasonal unsalted nuts: cashews, peanuts or sunflower seeds, but really any can be used)

1 teaspoon ground nutmeg

Steps

In a deep bowl, mix together flour, sugar and all other dry ingredients, including nuts, seeds and fruit. Make a hole in the center.

Melt shortening (or margarine) in a pot; add evaporated milk, egg and vanilla essence (warm slightly on stove top). Do not boil.

Add yeast to warm milk. Add milk mixture to flour (pour it in the center of the hole you created in the flour mixture). Mix with your clean hands until it holds together, knead and let rise for about 20 minutes or until dough swells up.

Knead again on a floured board.

Cut into 6-8 pieces.   Form into round balls or whatever shape and size you like. Flatten slightly. Put in greased baking pan. Let rise until doubled in size.

Preheat oven 350° to 375° F (180° C).

Bake for 30-40 minutes until brown all over or has hollow sound when tapped on the bottom. Cool on wire rack.

Pita Bread

Ingredients

3 cups all-purpose flour

1 teaspoon dry yeast

1 teaspoon salt

1 teaspoon sugar

1 ½ glass of lukewarm water

Steps

To prepare this pita bread recipe start by sifting the flour into your mixer's bowl. Add the yeast, sugar, salt, and combine with a spoon.

Add a little bit of water and start mixing, using the dough hook. Pour in the water a little bit at a time, at a steady stream, while mixing. Wait each time for the water to be absorbed and continue adding more as needed. Depending on the flour, the dough may need a little more or a bit less water than this pita bread recipe calls for.

After mixing for a while, the dough should become an elastic ball. If the dough is still crumbled, you should add some more water. If it becomes too sticky, this means that you added more water than needed. In that case, add 1 tsp of flour and continue mixing.

When done, cover the dough with a kitchen towel and let it sit in a warm place, for at least 20 minutes, until it doubles its size. This is an important step for this pita bread recipe, so that the pita bread becomes fluffy and soft.

Take the dough out of the bowl and knead a little bit. Split into 6-7 evenly sized portions.

To form the pita bread, you can either use a rolling pin, or stretch it with your hands, about 1 cm thick.

Heat a non-sticking frying pan to medium-high heat (no grease) and fry each pita bread for about 3-4 minutes on each side, until slightly colored and soft. To give more color, push down on the pita bread with a wooden spoon while in the pan.

If not consumed right away, wrap the pita bread in plastic wrap to keep it soft. Enjoy!

Dessert

Notes

Barazek

(Barazek is an Arabic dessert famous in Lebanon that is served with Turkish coffee or hot tea.)

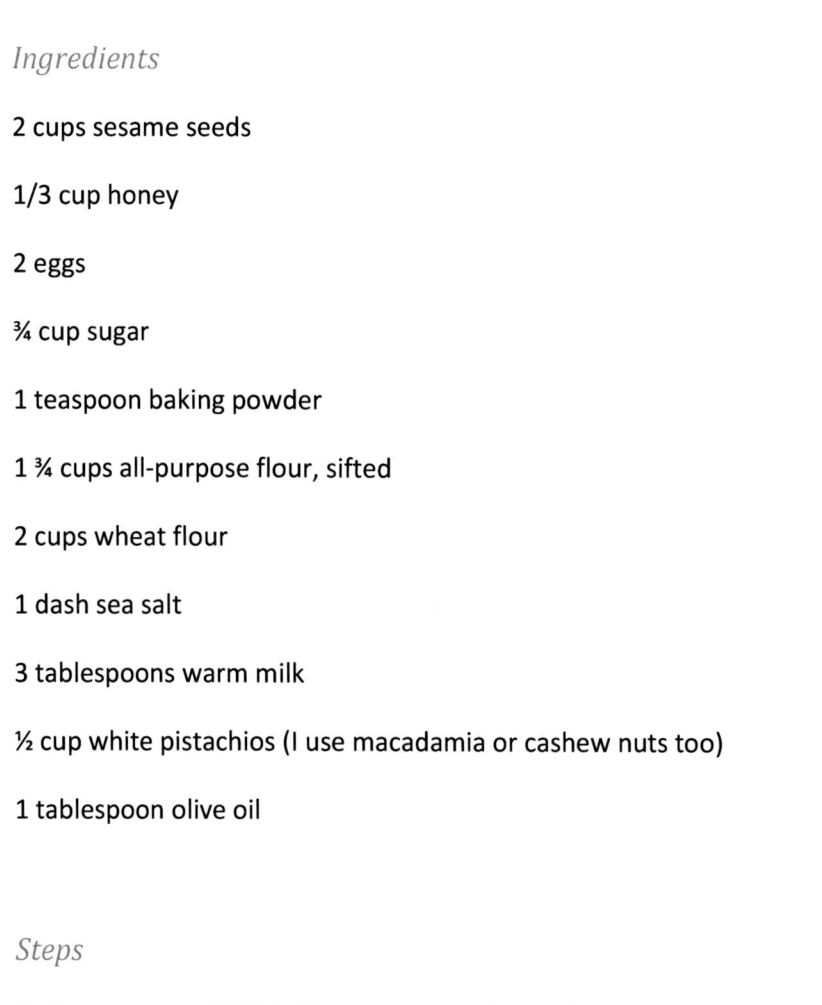

Ingredients

2 cups sesame seeds

1/3 cup honey

2 eggs

¾ cup sugar

1 teaspoon baking powder

1 ¾ cups all-purpose flour, sifted

2 cups wheat flour

1 dash sea salt

3 tablespoons warm milk

½ cup white pistachios (I use macadamia or cashew nuts too)

1 tablespoon olive oil

Steps

Preheat oven to 375° F. Mix sesame seeds with honey.

In an electric mixer, cream eggs, olive oil, and sugar together, until light and fluffy.

Sift the baking powder with the flour and salt; add to the egg mixture and blend thoroughly. Add milk gradually to form a dough.

Cut dough into small walnut-sized balls. Dip each ball into the pistachios, then flatten to form a 2-inch round cookie.

Place pistachio covered side face down on a greased cookie sheet. Cover each with 1 tablespoon of the sesame seed and honey mixture.

Bake for 15 minutes, or until golden.

Belizean Lemon Pie

Ingredients

Crust:

2 cups all-purpose flour

5 tablespoons vegetable shortening

½ teaspoon salt

6 to 7 tablespoons cold water, as needed

Filling and Topping:

5 eggs, separated

1 (14 ounce) can sweetened condensed milk

1 cup white sugar

1/3 to ½ cup lime juice, plus 1 teaspoon

1/8 teaspoon cream of tartar

Steps

For Crust:

Preheat oven to 400° F. Combine flour and salt. Cut in the shortening until coarse crumbs form. Add water, a little at a time, and stir until mixture forms a ball. Add sufficient water to get the dough to a rolling consistency. Flour your hands generously. Tilt the rolling pin and sprinkle it with flour as you rotate the rolling pin. On a lightly floured surface, form pastry into a ball; approximately 10 inches. Shape into a flattened round. Roll pastry 2 inches larger than an inverted pie plate with a floured rolling pin. Try to control the rolling pin and move from the center out. Don't use the rolling pin to go back and forth. Use your rolling pin something like this: Roll north, pick up the pin; roll northeast, pick up dough and move counter-clockwise; repeat. You want the crust as evenly rolled as possible.

Fold pastry into quarters and ease into a 9-inch pie plate, pressing firmly against bottom and sides of pie plate. Prick dough generously with a fork and bake for 15 to 20 minutes, or until crust is golden. Remove from oven and cool slightly. Set aside. Reduce oven to 350°F.

For Filling and Topping:

Beat egg yolks in a bowl until just mixed. Add condensed milk and combine. Add lime juice slowly, to desired taste (it should be a little tart). Pour into pie crust. Beat egg whites with electric mixer, on high, until foamy and thick. Reduce speed and slowly add 1 cup of sugar while continuing to beat. Increase to high until sugar is incorporated. Add 1 teaspoon of lime juice and cream of tartar and beat until thick peaks form. Spread on top of the egg yolk mixture. Be sure to spread the meringue so that it touches the pie crust, thereby forming a seal. Touch top of meringue with spatula to form peaks all over. Bake at 350° F for approximately 25 minutes, or until peaks are golden.

Pecan Pie

Ingredients

Crust:

1 cup butter or margarine, softened

2 (4 ounce) packages cream cheese, softened

2 cups flour

¼ cup sugar

Filling:

2 cups light corn syrup

1 ½ cups brown sugar, firmly packed

1/3 cup butter, melted

4 egg yolks, beaten

4 large eggs, lightly beaten

1 tablespoon vanilla extract

1/3 teaspoon salt

3 ½ cups pecan pieces or halves

Steps

For Crust:

Beat butter and cream cheese till creamy. Add flour and sugar gradually and mix until smooth.

Shape dough in a flat disk.

Refrigerate for at least 15 minutes.

For Filling:

Preheat oven to 375° F.

Combine filling ingredients in a deep bowl and mix together with a wire whisk.

Stretch chilled dough for crust out onto a pie pan and be sure it covers the sides. Pour filling into unbaked crust and cover with foil.

Bake for 15 minutes at 375° F

Then turn oven down to 300° F and continue to bake for 1 hour, or until pie is golden brown and the filling is of thick consistency. Cool and serve.

Sponge Cake

Ingredients

14 tablespoons caster sugar

14 tablespoons softened butter

4 eggs, beaten

14 tablespoons self-rising flour (if using regular flour add ½ teaspoon extra of baking powder)

1 teaspoon baking powder

2 tablespoons milk

1 drop Benjamin's pineapple essence

1 drop Benjamin's lemon essence

For the Filling:

3.5 ounces butter, softened

½ cup icing or powdered sugar, sifted

1 drop vanilla extract

1 cup of good quality strawberry jam (I use any flavor really)

Icing sugar, to decorate

Steps

Heat oven to 350º F. grease two 20 centimeter (8 inch) baking pans spray evenly with non-stick cooking spray. In a large bowl, beat all the cake ingredients together until you have a smooth, soft batter.

Divide the mixture between the tins, smooth the surface with a spatula or the back of a spoon, then bake for about 20 minutes until golden and the cake springs back when pressed gently. Turn onto a cooling rack and leave to cool completely.

To make the filling, beat the butter with an electric mixer, until smooth and creamy, then gradually beat in icing sugar. Beat in vanilla extract if you're using it. Spread the butter cream over the bottom of one of the sponges, top it with jam and sandwich the second sponge on top. Dust with a little icing sugar before serving. Keep in an airtight container and eat within 2 days.

Beverages

Notes

Iced Hibiscus Drink

Ingredients

1 cup fresh hibiscus petals

5 cups purified or mineral water

Sugar, to taste

Steps

Put the petals in a pan with water.

Bring to a boil and simmer for five minutes.

Add sugar to taste

Let cool, then filter into a jug; cover with plastic wrap, and chill.

Lemon and Rose Punch

Ingredients

1/3 cup fresh lemon juice

3 cups water

Sugar to taste

3 teaspoons rose water

A drop of pink food coloring (optional)

Mint leaves for garnish

Steps

Combine all ingredients (except mint leaves) in blender and blend for 30 to 60 seconds

Taste for sweetness

Leave in the fridge. Serve with ice and garnish with the mint leaves.

Middle Eastern Lemonade

Ingredients

8 lemons

¾ cup sugar, or to taste

¼ cup fresh mint, chopped

1 teaspoon orange blossom water

Water & ice cubes

Steps

Squeeze juice from the lemons in to a jar and sweeten with sugar, to taste.

Add the orange blossom water and mint, stir together.

Pour mixture to about one-third of a tall glass, then fill the glass with water and ice, to taste.

Notes

About the Author:

First time author, **Nefretery Nancy Marin**, lives in San Ignacio, Belize. She is a restaurateur and hospitality specialist, certified by the American Hotel and Lodging Educational Institute. She is also the owner of NMProductions Volunteer Corps & Medical Electives Belize and is well known for her philanthropic work with the children of Belize.

She inherited her enthusiasm for ethnic and cultural foods from her grandfather, Edwardo Juan (Hannah), who migrated to Belize from Lebanon in the early 1900's. Nancy enjoys traveling exclusively to search for her two passions, cultural foods and antiques.

Made in the USA
Columbia, SC
02 July 2023